GRIZZLY BEARS

Jack Ballard

FALCONGUIDES

GUILFORD, CONNECTICUT
HELENA MONTANA

© 2012 Rowman & Littlefield
ALL RIGHTS RESERVED. No part of this book may be reproduced or transmitted in any form by any means, electronic or mechanical, including photocopying and recording, or by any information storage and retrieval system, except as may be expressly permitted in writing from the publisher.

FalconGuides is an imprint of Globe Pequot Press.
Falcon, FalconGuides, and Outfit Your Mind are registered trademarks of Rowman & Littlefield.

Project editor: David Legere
Text design: Sheryl P. Kober
Layout: Sue Murray

Photos by Jack Ballard unless otherwise noted

Library of Congress Cataloging-in-Publication Data
Ballard, Jack (Jack Clayton)
 Grizzly bears / Jack Ballard.
   p. cm. — (A Falcon field guide)
 Includes bibliographical references and index.
 ISBN 978-0-7627-8003-7
1. Grizzly bear. 2. Grizzly bear—Identification. I. Title.
QL737.C27B3478 2012
 599.784—dc23
                              2012000192

Distributed by NATIONAL BOOK NETWORK

To Russ, whose tutelage in research design and interpretation
made this a better book.

Contents

Contents

Introduction

"Hey, Jack, come check this out."

At my companion's urging, I poke my head from the zippered door of a backpacking tent deep in the Absaroka-Beartooth Wilderness in Montana. It has snowed overnight, one of the hazards of camping in the high-elevation portions of the wilderness in September. I pull on my boots and a jacket and then scramble out of the tent. The sky above is blue and unclouded, the ground beneath my feet carpeted in 2 inches of snow. Weathered alpine grass pokes from the pale mantle. The gnarled evergreens behind our camp droop with snowflakes, sparkling, pure, and cheerful in the day's first bashful rays of sunlight.

As beautiful and pristine as are the surroundings, it isn't the scenery that Brad is so impatient to show me. Waving his arm from the open meadow 100 yards from our tent, he beckons me with an expression somewhere between a smile and a scowl. I jog toward him, noticing a line of tracks leading from the edge of the timber across the clearing. Silently he points at the prints. They appear somewhat similar to fat, barefoot tracks of a human, but one feature indelibly sets these apart from the footprints of any naked, deranged individual cavorting about the alpine zone in a snowstorm at 2 a.m. In front of the toes on the prints are claw marks measuring several inches in length. The identity of the nighttime visitor is obvious. Our camp was closely bypassed by a grizzly bear.

But the bruin had no interest in us, or in the food cache we suspended from a tree 150 yards from our camp, although with its keen sense of smell it was most certainly aware of the presence of both. Instinctively I shiver, with both fascination and fear.

Grizzly bears arouse similar emotions in other humans to whom they are known. Many of the terrors and trepidations aroused by these indomitable predators are unfounded or greatly overestimated. However, only a fool treads unthinkingly into their domain without a large measure of respect and preparation. For a century or more, grizzly bears in North America have been maligned and misunderstood. Misinformation has been haphazardly distributed by both individuals who would have people believe grizzlies are bloodthirsty man-eaters and those who have falsely portrayed them as gentle giants. I offer this book in hopes that it will expand both your appreciation for and knowledge of these iconic creatures of the American wilderness.

The author would like to thank Jamie Jonkel, bear biologist with the Montana Department of Fish, Wildlife, & Parks for reviewing and making helpful suggestions on the manuscript.

CHAPTER 1 Names and Faces

Names and Visual Description

Names of certain animals are based on their appearance. Such is the case of the "grizzly bear." Its coat is usually medium to dark brown in color. Long hairs, known as "guard hairs," adorn grizzly bears along the back and shoulders. Protruding beyond the dense undercoat, the guard hairs of a grizzly bear are pale or white-tipped, giving the animals a grizzled look. A term historically used for the graying of hair on the human head, "grizzle" means to become gray or white. Early observers apparently likened the light guard hairs on grizzly bears to gray highlights in human hair. Thus, the name "grizzly bear" stems from the pale highlights in the dark coat of this large bear. In some locations this unique coloration on grizzly bears gave rise to another name, the "silvertip bear," a historical term not commonly encountered in modern terminology. Captain Meriwether Lewis of the Lewis and Clark expedition sometimes referred to the grizzly bear as the "white bear" in his journals, evidently in reference to the light hair on upper portions of a grizzly bear's body.

As previously mentioned, the typical coat of a grizzly bear appears as brown. However, individual bears can exhibit color variations ranging from light tan to nearly black. The extent of the grizzling varies as well. Some bears, viewed in the sunlight, almost seem to shine with radiance, a spectacle that gave rise to one of the grizzly bear's nicknames, the "silvertip." Other bears show minimal grizzling. These animals appear more solidly colored in whatever shade of brown is exhibited by a particular animal. For the purposes of species identification, the trademark pale hairs on the back and shoulders of a grizzly bear are one clue of its species, but not a definitive field mark.

Adult grizzly bears are large animals with a noticeable hump over their front shoulders when viewed from the side. The hump is composed of a muscular mass that facilitates the

Grizzly bears are named for the light hairs on their head and shoulders and the light highlights in their darker coat that give them a "grizzled" appearance. Photo Kevin Rhoades

animals' excellent digging capabilities with the forepaws and their running speed. Their rump slopes away from the back in a rounded arc. Like other bears, grizzlies have a small tail that is often unnoticeable except when viewed from certain angles. Grizzly bears have massive front paws. Large claws extend from each foot and are often easy to see on the front paws. The claws of grizzly bears are longer and straighter than those of black bears, usually measuring 2 to 4 inches in length.

The face of the grizzly bear appears large and rounded when viewed head-on. Seen from the side, the face of a grizzly looks slightly concave or dished. Grizzlies have short ears that often look tiny in relation to the mass of the head on adult animals. The end of a grizzly bear's nose is black.

Naming of genders within grizzly bears follows the pattern of a poorly esteemed barnyard animal. Male grizzlies are known as "boars." Females are called "sows." Despite their iconic status as wilderness creatures, male and female grizzlies carry the same gender identities as pigs. However, youngsters of these regal predators fare much better in the naming category. They're not called piglets, but are referred to as "cubs."

Related Species in North America

Three species of bears are indigenous to North America: grizzly bears, black bears, and polar bears. Black bears *(Ursus americanus)* inhabit much of the same range as grizzly bears, except in the extreme northern reaches of Alaska and Canada, where grizzlies are present but not black bears. The two species are often confused by uneducated observers. Not all black bears are black in color. Like grizzlies, their coloration can vary quite dramatically, from nearly white to coal black. Although black is the dominant color of black bears, other colorations that are highly similar to the basic color scheme of grizzly bears occur. "Blonde" and "cinnamon" color phases of black bears are virtually identical to the hues found on the coats of many grizzlies. And remember, grizzly bears can be very dark. Thus, coloration is a very poor way to distinguish black bears from grizzly bears.

Grizzly bears share portions of their range in North America with black bears and polar bears. Grizzly bears have a prominent shoulder hump and dished face not seen on black or polar bears. PHOTO WILLIAM MULLINS

To the trained eye, the size of adult bears is one means of separating black bears from grizzlies. The average mature grizzly bear commonly weighs twice as much as the normal black bear, or even more. However, there are more certain ways to distinguish the species than color and size. Black bears lack the noticeable hump on the front shoulders that marks the grizzly. Their ears appear much longer in relation to their head than those of a grizzly bear. Viewed from the side, the concave appearance of the face of a grizzly bear is absent from a black bear. A black bear has a face that is straight or somewhat convex or slightly rounded outward. The claws of a black bear are not nearly as large or easily seen as those on a grizzly. When startled or alarmed, black bears may bolt up a tree, an evasive strategy not likely employed by an adult grizzly bear. Rather than relying on a single trait such as color to distinguish between black bears and grizzlies, one can make a more certain identification by analyzing a particular animal for a variety of distinguishing features.

Black bear or grizzly? Although this bear has retained a shock of light hair on its shoulders from its winter coat, its large ears and lack of a shoulder hump indicate that it's a black bear.

In addition to black bears, grizzlies share the North American continent with polar bears *(Ursus maritimus)*. Residents of the far north, polar bears are found on the ice packs in the extreme northern reaches of Canada, Alaska, and the Arctic Islands. In a few places the range of polar bears and grizzly bears overlap. In the areas of overlap, the habitat is usually not ideal for grizzlies. Few grizzly bears have historically ranged into areas also inhabited by polar bears.

In addition to the obvious differences in range, the appearance of polar bears and grizzly bears is quite distinct. Polar bears are uniformly white in color, often mingled with yellowish tones. A polar bear has short ears like the grizzly, but its profile exhibits a straight face more like the black bear than the dished appearance of the grizzly. Their claws are sharp, allowing them excellent traction on ice, but are much smaller and less noticeable than those on a grizzly bear. On average, polar bears are larger than the grizzly bears that inhabit interior regions of North America.

Polar bears are even more carnivorous than grizzly bears. While grizzlies contentedly dine on a variety of plants, nuts, and berries, such food sources are absent on the frozen ice packs. Polar bears dine primarily upon seals, young walruses, and fish.

Subspecies

Discussing the subspecies of grizzly bears raises an interesting point. Technically, there are no subspecies of grizzly bears. In fact, the grizzly bear is thought to be a subspecies by many biologists. Grizzly bears belong to the species *Ursus arctos,* which also includes the Alaskan brown bear. From a scientific standpoint both Alaskan brown bears and grizzly bears belong to the *Ursus arctos* species.

Subspecies of mammals are defined as unique, identifiable populations with genetic, physical, or social characteristics that separate them from the species as a whole.

In North America the brown bear is sometimes described as consisting of two subspecies, the Alaskan brown bear or

Kodiak bear *(Ursus arctos middendorffi)* and the grizzly bear *(Ursus arctos horribilis)*. In the past century other categories of subspecies have also been proposed, some identifying a half-dozen different subspecies. However, the nomenclature relating to the brown bear species is often confusing. Some authoritative biologists refer to the entire *Ursus arctos* species as "grizzly bears," while others stick with "brown bears." For common folks it appears this is one species where you can choose a name. Take your pick. Whether you refer to these dominating predators as brown bears or grizzly bears, you're on sound scientific footing.

What distinguishes Alaskan brown bears from grizzly bears? For most biologists Alaskan brown bears, or the subspecies *Ursus arctos middendorffi,* refer to the population found along the coasts and islands of southern Alaska. Members of the robust population of these bears roaming Kodiak Island are sometimes known as Kodiak brown bears or Kodiak bears. While these coastal-dwelling bears were once deemed a separate species, biologists now recognize them merely as a subspecies of brown bears or make no distinction at all between this coastal population and bears ranging the interior of the continent.

Access to a rich diet of fish at certain times of the year, primarily spawning salmon, allows the Alaskan brown bear to reach an extraordinarily large size. Males often weigh in excess of 1,000 pounds, with exceptionally large specimens attaining over 1,500 pounds in weight. These gargantuan creatures are roughly equivalent in size to huge male polar bears, making them (along with male polar bears) the most massive land-dwelling carnivores on earth. Purported weights of both male Alaskan brown bears and polar bears have exceeded an incredible 1,700 pounds, nearly as large as a fully mature male bison or domestic bull!

Brown bears roaming the interior of the North American continent belong to the *Ursus arctos horribilis* subspecies and are commonly known as grizzly bears. As for some other mammals, the size of grizzly bears generally follows Bergmann's rule, a

A rich diet allows grizzly bears dwelling on the coastline of the Pacific Ocean in places such as Alaska's Katmai National Park to achieve extraordinarily large sizes.
Photo William Mullins

biological postulate that concludes that the mass of animals within a species increases in colder or more northern climates. Thus, the largest specimens for species such as moose, whitetail deer, and gray wolves come from the northern populations. While this rule (more like a trend) doesn't apply to all creatures, it holds quite true in relation to grizzly bears. Animals found in the northern interior of Alaska and Canada are considerably larger, on average, than those roaming the grizzlies' southernmost range in Idaho, Montana, and Wyoming.

Physical Characteristics

Grizzly bears, depending on their sex and range, exhibit a remarkable range in size. Smaller females in the southern portion of the bears' range may weigh just slightly over 300 pounds, while northern or coastal females can attain over twice that weight, up to nearly 800 pounds. Males usually weigh from 500 to 1,000 pounds. As noted earlier, exceptionally large males in coastal Alaskan populations may burgeon to over 1,500 pounds. Measured at the front shoulder, grizzlies range from around 3.5 to 4.5 feet in height when on all fours. Their body length commonly stretches from about 6 to 8.5 feet from tail to nose. Large males sometimes exceed these measurements for both height and length by considerable margins. Grizzlies sometimes stand on their hind legs, apparently to obtain a better perception of the world around them. An erect adult grizzly often stands from 7 to 8 feet in height. Standing height of the largest males can exceed 10 feet, with some individuals estimated as having heights greater than 12 feet. For the sake of comparison, the regulation height of a basketball rim is 10 feet. If it were taught to play the game, I doubt any human all-star alive could dunk over a big boar grizzly!

The hind foot of a very large grizzly may measure 16 inches long by 10 inches wide, although most prints are somewhat smaller, around 10 inches long and 6 inches wide, depending on the location and size of the bear. A grizzly's hind feet are slightly larger than its front feet. The tracks are wide but elongated,

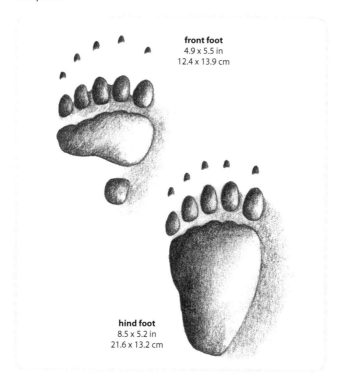

front foot
4.9 x 5.5 in
12.4 x 13.9 cm

hind foot
8.5 x 5.2 in
21.6 x 13.2 cm

appearing somewhat like a broad barefoot human print with noticeable claw marks.

Utilized for digging, defense, and subduing prey, the claws of an adult grizzly bear may reach 4 inches in length. Although awkward appearing when walking with its head swinging lazily from side to side, a mature grizzly is remarkably swift and agile. The bears can sprint at speeds of 30 miles per hour or slightly faster, a speed that rivals the pace of the average horse in full gallop. Historical information from Yellowstone National Park from the late 1930s records grizzly bears comfortably running for over 2 miles at 25 miles per hour. The same record notes that

Grizzly bear tracks are elongated, with noticeable toe prints and claw marks.
PHOTO KEVIN RHOADES

Although awkward appearing, grizzly bears can run as fast as the average horse.
PHOTO SHUTTERSTOCK

grizzly bears can keep up with horses running downhill, but are outdistanced when following horses uphill. This observation might have given rise to the erroneous notion that humans attempting to flee from a bear are better served running uphill instead of downhill. In fact, grizzly bears are so much faster than humans that fleeing in any direction is futile.

WHAT ABOUT THE PIZZLY?

On April 16, 2006, a hunter shot a polar bear on Banks Island in the Northwest Territories of Canada. The bear's white fur was mottled with patches of brown. It had a concave face, sported a hump on its shoulders, and had very long claws, physical attributes commonly associated with grizzly bears. Wildlife officials seized the animal. DNA tests revealed that the bear was the offspring of a male grizzly and a female polar bear. What do you call such a creature? Several names have been proposed. Locals in the area in which the hybrid grizzly-polar bear was killed have suggested "pizzly bear" or "grolar bear." Canadian wildlife officials have another idea. Combining the Inuit names for polar bear *(nanuk)* and grizzly bear *(aklak)*, wildlife officials believe "nanulak" is the most appropriate moniker for an animal that weds parentage of these two species of bears.

While the bear taken in 2006 confirms that grizzly bears and polar bears do sometimes interbreed in the wild, other evidence has suggested this possibility for many decades. Anecdotal reports of Alaskan or Canadian hunters killing bears with white fur interspersed with brown have circulated for some time. In the nineteenth century brown bears and polar bears successfully mated in zoos in England and Germany. At the United States National Zoo in 1936, a male polar bear inadvertently made its way into an enclosure housing a female Alaskan brown bear. Their mating yielded three cubs that grew to adulthood and mated successfully. These instances clearly demonstrated that polar bears and grizzly bears could mate and produce offspring. But given the fact that the bears' habitats overlap in few areas and that the two species are usually aggressive toward one another, some biologists previously believed that successful mating of the two species in the wild was unlikely.

Even if polar bears and grizzly bears mate and rear young, how capable will the offspring be of surviving and propagating? Hybrids of some species tend to get the worst of both worlds, so to speak, not the best. Mule deer and whitetail deer hybridize on rare occasions. However, their offspring display neither the bouncing gait of the mule deer nor the bounding gait of the whitetail, making them more vulnerable to predators than either parent, or so some biologists believe.

Evidently, grizzly-polar bear hybrids aren't completely incapable of survival and reproduction. In 2010 a native Inuvialuit hunter shot a second-generation hybrid bear. Genetic analysis of the animal determined it was the offspring of a female hybrid and a male grizzly.

Hybridization of the two species raises questions on many fronts. First of all, if the two species can interbreed and produce fertile offspring, shouldn't they be classified as a single species? Some biologists would argue yes; others no. Genetic modeling suggests that polar bears and grizzly bears descended from a common ancestor. Theorists believe that some 125,000 years ago a segment of the brown bear population in the northern extreme of their range was isolated by huge glaciers. Through natural selection these bears eventually developed the white coat and physical adaptations that allow them to hunt seals and other marine animals in the Arctic.

If polar bears and grizzlies descended from a common ancestor, could more frequent interbreeding once again meld the separate species into one? This question isn't of much concern to grizzlies, which have a greater range and broader diet. But some biologists worry that the melting of the polar ice pack due to global warming might threaten the survival of polar bears. Interbreeding with grizzlies would further jeopardize the identity of these great white hunters of the north. While these concerns may vex those who champion the purity of the polar bear species, it seems there's little to do but watch—and try to decide which name is better, "pizzly" or "grolar."

CHAPTER 2

Range and Habitat

Historic Range

Ask the average person where grizzly bears live and you'll probably hear some variation of a three-word answer: in the mountains. While that observation is true, grizzlies also roam across open expanses of tundra in the far north. Although it may come as a surprise to many people, grizzly bears are as suited to living on the plains as in the mountains. Prior to European settlement of North America, these great bears were common residents on the Great Plains, where they hunted bison and elk alongside wolves.

Members of the Lewis and Clark expedition encountered grizzly bears far east of the Rocky Mountains on their westward

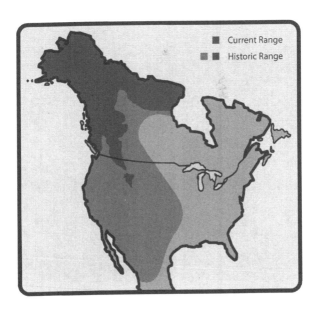

trek to the Pacific coast. In April 1805, as the explorers journeyed through central and western North Dakota along the Missouri River, they discovered tracks of "the white bear of enormous size" and sighted a few grizzlies. After subsequent encounters in eastern Montana, where the corps learned that grizzlies were incredibly fast, unpredictable, and extremely hard to kill, grizzly bears became one of the most feared hazards of the journey. The U.S. Fish and Wildlife Service (USFWS) estimates that around 50,000 grizzly bears roamed the western United States at the time of the Lewis and Clark expedition, ranging from the Pacific Ocean to the Great Plains.

As settlers moved onto the plains and into the Rocky Mountains, grizzly bears were eliminated through hunting and trapping. Prior to the animals' extermination by humans, the large, clawed footprints of grizzly bears marked the soil in the interior of

A grizzly bear adorns the state flag of California. Grizzlies were historically present in the state, but were eliminated in the 1920s. Photo Shutterstock

what is now the United States as far east as Ohio. Grizzlies were also present in the coastal mountain ranges along the Pacific Ocean, ranging southward through California and into northern Mexico. A grizzly bear adorns the state flag of California, although the last surviving member of the state's historic population was killed in 1922. East of California these mighty bears roamed across the American Southwest at least as far east as central Texas.

By 1922 biologists were aware of only thirty-seven intact grizzly bear populations in the contiguous United States. In 1975, when grizzly bears in the lower forty-eight states received protection as a "threatened species" under the Endangered Species Act, only six of those thirty-seven populations remained.

In the north historic grizzly bear populations spanned a range from the western coastline of Alaska eastward to the western shores of Hudson Bay in Canada and everywhere in between. Grizzly bears were found in abundance in the western provinces of Canada, namely British Columbia and Alberta.

Current Range

Currently, grizzly bears are found in the greatest numbers in Alaska and western Canada. They also range across northern Canada in the Yukon and Northwest Territories and Nunavut. An estimated 30,000 or more grizzly bears inhabit Alaska. Canada's grizzly bear population is estimated at 26,000 animals, nearly half of which are found in British Columbia.

In the contiguous United States, members of this species are known to inhabit Washington, Idaho, Montana, and Wyoming. Within those four states grizzly bears definitively occupy five ecosystems identified by the USFWS. In Washington State grizzlies inhabit the north-central portion in the North Cascade Mountains. This area is known as the North Cascades recovery zone for grizzly bear management. The area includes remote, mountainous terrain in and around North Cascades National Park. Bears living in this area also inhabit contiguous habitat in southern British Columbia. At the present time the USFWS estimates there are fewer than twenty grizzlies in the portion of this ecosystem

Alaska and western Canada have the highest concentrations of grizzly bears in North America, many of which live in coastal areas. Photo William Mullins

that lies within the United States, with perhaps another two dozen bruins in British Columbia. Given the limited number of bears in the area, most biologists feel this remnant population of grizzly bears faces low odds of survival without intense recovery efforts, which could include population augmentation with bears transplanted from other areas.

Given the extremely small population of grizzlies that ranges across the 9,500-square-mile North Cascades recovery zone, efforts to observe and study the bears often meet with failure. However, random encounters with grizzlies in the area attest to their survival. In late October 2009 a hiker snapped a few photos of a grizzly bear he encountered while hiking in the upper reaches of the Cascade River drainage. The photos came to light in the public eye in 2010. At the time, some wildlife officials believed grizzly bears had abandoned the North Cascades portion of the United States. However, given the bear's location, biologists concluded it wasn't likely a transient bear from Canada, but a bruin that resided in the United States. Though precarious, the population of grizzly bears in the North Cascades is apparently still viable.

East of the North Cascades, grizzly bears are also found in Washington state in the Selkirk Mountains north of Spokane, a population area that also includes the extreme northern portion of Idaho. This grizzly bear recovery area includes 2,200 square miles, an area just smaller than the state of Delaware. Similar to the North Cascades ecosystem, grizzly bear habitat in the Selkirk Mountains runs northward into Canada.

The Selkirk ecosystem has distinct boundaries. On the north and east sides, Kootenay Lake (British Columbia) and the Kootenai River (Idaho) form natural geographic boundaries. On the south and east sides, the Selkirk ecosystem finds its limits at the Salmo River (British Columbia) and the Pend Oreille River (Washington and Idaho). The Selkirk ecosystem is home to an estimated forty to fifty grizzly bears, based on data published by the USFWS. Human-caused mortality appears to be the greatest inhibitor to growth of this grizzly bear population. Of the grizzly bear deaths recorded in the period from 1983 to 2002, a full 80 percent were human caused. A small percentage of the bears were misidentified by hunters legally hunting black bears. Others were removed by wildlife managers after becoming "problem bears" that strayed into small towns, raided campsites or cabins, or engaged in other activities that threatened humans. A few bears were killed by illegal hunting activities (poaching).

Not far east of the Selkirk Mountains lies a third recovery zone for grizzly bears. Known as the Cabinet-Yaak recovery zone, this area encompasses 2,600 square miles of habitat that lies primarily in northwestern Montana, but also extends westward into the Idaho Panhandle. The Cabinet-Yaak ecosystem is divided into two distinct segments by the Kootenai River in northwestern Montana. The Yaak River segment of this recovery area lies north of the

Misidentification by humans hunting black bears accounts for grizzly bear deaths in Montana and other states. Subadult grizzlies (like these two) are most often mistakenly targeted by hunters.

Kootenai River, the Cabinet Mountain portion to the south. The Cabinet Mountain portion of the ecosystem composes roughly 60 percent of the total area and includes the Cabinet Mountain Wilderness. Grizzly bear habitat extends from the Cabinet-Yaak portion of the United States northward into Canada.

The USFWS estimates that thirty to forty grizzly bears inhabit the Cabinet-Yaak recovery zone. Human-caused mortality was lower in the Cabinet-Yaak recovery zone in the 1983 to 2002 time period than in the Selkirk zone, although around 50 percent of the bears in the research study that died were killed as a result of humans. Most of the deaths occurred within a relatively short distance of a road, a trend similarly recorded in the Selkirk recovery zone. This factor points to a key principle in maintaining grizzly bear habitat. The bears do best in areas where they're buffered from frequent encounters with people and the trappings of human civilization.

Moving eastward into northern Montana, the Northern Continental Divide recovery area includes Glacier National Park, the Bob Marshall Wilderness Complex, and adjacent areas. Grizzly habitat associated with this ecosystem (also known as the NCDE) extends northward into Canada. This area is home to one of the largest populations of grizzly bears in the contiguous United States. A five-year study completed in 2008 using DNA samples from hair-snagging stations and bear rubs in the NCDE revealed samples from 563 individual bears. Undertaken by a team of over 200 researchers and assistants from the Northern Divide Grizzly Bear Project, statistical analysis of the data to account for bears not sampled in the project indicates that slightly more than 750 bears roamed the NCDE at the close of the study. The population has been increasing, with bears moving from the recovery zone into adjacent areas. Similar to other parts of the country, grizzly conflicts and mortality are highest in the NCDE where bears routinely come into contact with humans. Less than 20 percent of the land area in this recovery zone is owned by private entities. However, private land accounts for the highest percentage of human-bear conflicts and bear deaths.

The most well-known population of grizzly bears in the contiguous United States ranges across an area encompassing Yellowstone National Park and adjacent wildlands. Known as the Greater Yellowstone Ecosystem, this region includes several wilderness areas in addition to Yellowstone National Park. Grizzly bears in this area are also found in Grand Teton National Park in Wyoming. Bears are found as far east as the northwestern portion of the Wind River Indian Reservation in Wyoming and westward along the Montana-Idaho divide to a point roughly 50 miles west of Yellowstone National Park. The bears have expanded their range from a core area around Yellowstone to the Bridger-Teton National Forest south of Grand Teton National Park in Wyoming, the Targhee National Forest on the west side of the Teton Range in Idaho, and the Beaverhead-Deerlodge National Forest west of Yellowstone National Park in Montana.

In 2007 the USFWS declared this growing grizzly population to be recovered, no longer meeting endangered or threatened status as defined by the Endangered Species Act. However, an order issued in 2009 from the federal district court in Missoula,

Montana, overturned the delisting of the grizzly bears in the Yellowstone area, returning them to protection under the Endangered Species Act, a status they have carried since 1975. Regardless of the bears' position under the Endangered Species Act, grizzly bears are doing well in the Yellowstone recovery area. When they were listed as a threatened species in the lower forty-eight states in 1975, an estimated 136 grizzly bears were found in the Yellowstone recovery area. Current population estimates exceed 500 animals. Yearly population increases of grizzly bears in the Yellowstone area have been as high as 7 percent. Biologists from a multi-agency team of researchers have concluded that more than 600 of these great brown bears roam the wildlands in and around Yellowstone National Park. The researchers note

The area in and around Yellowstone National Park harbors the highest number of grizzly bears in the lower forty-eight states. Yellowstone's grizzly bear population has been growing in recent years due to good cub production and survival.

that their population estimate is very conservative, making it possible that the number of bears actually living in the area is significantly higher.

When the grizzly bear was listed as a threatened species under the Endangered Species Act, a sixth recovery area was identified, though it was believed to be void of grizzly bears. The Bitterroot recovery zone spans 5,600 square miles of habitat in east-central Idaho and western Montana, including two large wilderness areas: the Selway-Bitterroot Wilderness area on the Idaho-Montana divide (west of Hamilton, Montana) and the Frank Church Wilderness (west of Salmon, Idaho). Preliminary plans to reintroduce grizzly bears into the Bitterroot recovery area were eventually abandoned by the USFWS. Although the USFWS took an official position that bears were absent from the ecosystem and proposed a reintroduction program in 1997, the reintroduction plan was withdrawn as a proposal in 2001. Opposition to the reintroduction plan came on several fronts. Some local residents opposed having grizzly bears in the area under any plan. Others believed that grizzly bears did inhabit the area and were concerned that a reintroduced population would not be afforded the same federal protections as native bears. Grizzly bears are evidently taking matters into their own hands. A black bear hunter accidentally shot a young male grizzly in September 2007 while hunting in the northern end of the Bitterroot recovery zone. Since then several other grizzly bear encounters have clearly established that bears are present in or very near the recovery zone. Many of these animals have been young males, a segment of the population much more likely to wander than older males or breeding-age females. However, many experts now believe grizzly bears will recolonize this expanse of rugged habitat on their own.

Grizzly Bear Habitat

For all living species, food, water, secure places to rest, and adequate physical space to occupy are the essential elements of habitat. The current state of habitat in relation to grizzly bears is somewhat artificial. Grizzly bears are capable of living in some habitats (such as the Great Plains) that they no longer occupy because their presence is incompatible with agriculture and human civilization.

In the lower forty-eight states, grizzly bears primarily roam across alpine and subalpine forests. They occupy similar habitat in the mountains of western Canada and Alaska. Where bears are present along the Pacific coast of Alaska and Canada, they're often found near streams where they prey upon fish, primarily spawning salmon. At the northernmost portions of their range, in Alaska, the Yukon, Northwest Territories, and Nunavut, grizzly bears make their living in the open tundra.

Grizzly bear females, with or without cubs, require a smaller home range than males.

The amount of space required as habitat for individual grizzly bears varies remarkably depending upon their gender and the geographic area in which they live. Whether it's Grand Teton National Park in Wyoming or Katmai National Park in Alaska or any other location occupied by bears, male grizzlies require much more space than females. The average home range of a boar is two to ten times larger than that of a mature sow living in the same area. Scientists believe the larger ranges of males are related to two primary factors. First, a larger space gives a male higher odds of finding and mating with females. Second, the larger body size of males necessitates a higher protein and caloric intake to maintain, requiring males to range over a more expansive area in search of food. It is important to remember that grizzly bears technically occupy a home range, not a territory. In biological terms a "territory" refers to a segment of land occupied by an animal where other animals of the same species or gender are expelled. Grizzly bears are not territorial in this sense. The range of several males and females may overlap, even though individual bears have preferred areas.

Just how large is a grizzly bear's home range? One research study involving twelve female bears on Admiralty Island, Alaska, showed an average size of slightly more than 9 square miles. Another study that recorded the movements of nineteen male bears in the central Northwest Territories of Canada yielded an average home range occupying just over 3,150 square miles, a land area significantly larger than the state of Delaware. Individual grizzly bear males in the open tundra of north-central Canada are believed to have ranges as large as 10,000 square miles, an area 100 miles wide by 100 miles long, or slightly larger than the state of Vermont. A grizzly bear's home range is highly correlated to forage. Bears occupying areas with access to abundant, high-quality food sources (such as salmon) have much smaller ranges than those living in areas where forage is less plentiful.

HABITAT FRAGMENTATION

Grizzly bears thrive in large tracts of wilderness or roadless habitat where they're buffered from routine disturbance by humans and their vehicles. However, such areas are the exception, not the rule, in the contiguous United States and much of southwestern Canada. Furthermore, regions of wilderness habitat are often "islands" surrounded by private land or public lands where human activities such as logging, mining, and agriculture abound.

In such areas habitats that could potentially support grizzly bears are isolated from one another. Known as "habitat fragmentation" in biological circles, this phenomenon affects not only grizzly bears but other creatures such as lynx, wolverines, and bighorn sheep. Habitat fragmentation makes

it difficult for grizzly bears to expand their range through the natural process of species dispersion as one region of habitat reaches its "carrying capacity." Young bears, incapable of claiming a territory in the area of their birth, are prime candidates to move into unpopulated regions. However, if such movement requires navigating a course across roads, through river valleys occupied by agriculture or areas of high human population, the odds of a young bear making it to another area of unoccupied habitat are severely diminished. Thus, preserving habitat for grizzly bears not only includes managing a suitable amount of land area for the bears, it also means ensuring that sufficiently wild "corridors" connect larger chunks of habitat to avoid fragmentation.

Roads fragment grizzly bear habitat and sometimes create impediments to the dispersal of young adult bears seeking new territories.

CHAPTER 3 Forage and Nutritional Requirements

Basic Food Sources and Digestive Biology

The sheer size of a grizzly bear demands a considerable intake of nutrition to maintain. Large bears feeding actively may consume eighty to ninety pounds of forage per day. Grizzly bears newly emerged from their dens in the spring don't consume as much forage as they do in the fall prior to denning in the winter. After hibernation it takes the digestive system of a bear a period of time to reaccustom itself to food intake after a long period of dormancy.

Plants, particularly young, tender grasses and leafy plants, make up a high percentage of the diet of a grizzly bear.

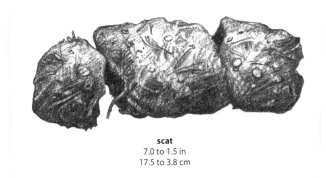

scat
7.0 to 1.5 in
17.5 to 3.8 cm

Contrary to the beliefs of many people, grizzly bears are not primarily meat-eaters. However, it's difficult to make sound generalizations about the diet of grizzly bears because their eating habits vary drastically based on the time of year and the region of the continent in which they live. Like other carnivores (including humans), bears have a digestive system that includes a single stomach. Their intestines are fairly short. The digestive system of a grizzly bear processes food quite quickly. Meat clears the digestive tract in about 13 hours, while tender plants such as clover may be digested in as little as 7 hours. Although most grizzly bears eat plant matter as a high percentage of their diet, they are very selective herbivores. Lacking the ability to digest plant stalks efficiently, bears favor young, tender grasses and leafy plants that break down more easily than mature grasses or woody plants.

The mouth and teeth of a grizzly bear facilitate its eclectic diet. Their canine teeth are sharp enough to aid them in catching and killing prey. However, their molars are much more developed for chewing than those of carnivores from the feline and canine families, allowing them to efficiently eat and digest plant material.

Grizzly bears are highly omnivorous, meaning they eat both plants and animals. Compared to polar bears, grizzlies eat less meat and more plants. Compared to black bears, grizzlies eat more meat, making them the most omnivorous of the North American bears. However, the percentage of meat in a grizzly bear's diet is highly variable. In general, grizzly bears that inhabit the coastal regions of Alaska or have access to spawning salmon consume a much higher percentage of meat than those living in the interior of the continent. Research indicates that bears with access to salmon may consume as much as 75 percent or more of their diet in meat. By contrast, bears roaming areas without salmon, such as Montana's Glacier National Park, may live on a diet consisting of less than 10 percent meat.

Along the coast of Alaska and some other locations, grizzly bears consume a high percentage of their diet in meat, most of it spawning salmon. This grizzly sow has caught a silver salmon at Lake Clark National Park in Alaska. Photo William Mullins

So what do all grizzly bears eat? The best answer to that question is "Whatever is edible and available." A grizzly bear's digestive system can handle about anything, from wasps to mushrooms to the decaying carcass of a winter-killed bison to a simple blade of grass.

Following the system of humans eating from four food groups, the diet of grizzly bears can be similarly analyzed. Let's call the first category vegetables. This would include some grasses that bears commonly eat in the springtime by grazing. Bears also eat forbs (leafy plants), along with portions of plants that grow beneath the soil: roots, corms, and bulbs. Biscuitroot, glacier lily, sweetvetch, and yampa provide grizzlies in some areas with important sources of nutrition that come from the below-ground portions of the plants. The long claws of grizzly bears enable them to efficiently excavate large patches of soil in search of these root crops.

A second category of grizzly food is fruit. This includes primarily berries. These high-calorie fruits are gleaned from shrubs. Huckleberries, blueberries, buffaloberries, rose hips, and bearberries are all important fruits for grizzly bears. In some areas they may eat chokecherries and raspberries as well.

Nuts are a third category of grizzly grub. One nut in particular comprises this food group. Where available, grizzly bears feed voraciously on the nuts of the whitebark pine tree. Whitebark pine cones are loaded with nuts and the trees are loaded with cones in years with good precipitation. Whitebark pine nuts are most important to grizzly bears in the northern Rocky Mountain region of the contiguous United States in such places as Grand Teton and Yellowstone National Parks. Although many grizzlies in these areas feed extensively on whitebark pine nuts, they don't do the work of harvesting them. Bears most commonly raid the extensive caches of pine nuts gathered by red squirrels.

The final category included in the grizzly diet is meat. This category includes the normal creatures people expect grizzly bears to prey upon, such as elk, moose, deer, and caribou. However, grizzly bears are also known to expend considerable energy and effort to dig voles and small ground squirrels from their burrows.

DROUGHT, DISEASE, AND DIET

Grizzly bears are large, powerful predators. By all appearances it seems they're supreme masters of their own destiny. After all, an animal capable of snuffing out the life of a deer or wolf with a single blow of its forepaw can certainly take care of itself. Or can it?

Grizzly bears need to pack on considerable fat reserves to survive during hibernation. Large male bears, be they the gargantuan coastal specimens or the smaller but still impressively powerful boars prowling the interior of the continent, require a considerable caloric intake from the time they wake up in the spring until they hibernate in the fall.

As with primitive human farmers of old, the dietary well-being of grizzly bears is highly influenced by the whims of nature. For the bears inhabiting the northern Rocky Mountains in eastern Washington, Idaho, and northern Montana, a bumper huckleberry crop means easy autumn living and lots of body fat to survive the winter. If the berry crop fails due to drought, an important food source may all but vanish. In Yellowstone National Park prodigious production of whitebark pine nuts has similar consequences. However, disease and beetle infestations are now serious threats to the health of the pine trees. In the future, even years of favorable cone production may mean fewer nuts for grizzly bears, forcing them to find other fall food sources than the high-calorie nuts.

Coastal grizzly bears that feed upon salmon might seem to have an easier life. However, harvest by human anglers, changes in ocean habitat, and competition from other predators such as birds and sea lions may substantially reduce the number of fish available to grizzly bears. Unknown factors affect the salmon run as well. Some years the fish come in abundance, but at other times there are fewer, for reasons no one can fully explain.

By preserving habitat and offering grizzly bears plenty of space to roam in which they encounter few conflicts with people, humans can help create conditions that ensure their health and survival. But the same systems, cycles, and exceptions in nature affecting the well-being of creatures as tiny as the red squirrel also impact those as mighty as the grizzly bear.

For grizzlies like this one in Denali National Park, fall is a critical, but sometimes unpredictable, season in the yearly forage cycle. Photo Shutterstock

They will also eat earthworms and wasp nests. In certain locations in Glacier and Yellowstone National Parks, moths are an extremely important source of meat (can you imagine seeing "moth meat" on a menu?) for grizzly bears. Grizzly bears acquire their "moth meat" from hundreds of thousands of moths that sometimes roost in rockslides in remote, high-elevation locations. Rounding out the meat category is fish. While salmon are the fish species most commonly consumed by grizzly bears, they will also happily dine upon trout and other species when available.

Forage Preferences by the Seasons

Nature's yearly cycle of seasons significantly affects the types of foods available to grizzly bears no matter where they live. Before the advent of refrigeration and modern transportation, the diets of humans were also more significantly influenced by seasonal cycles than they are today. Americans can pop into a grocery store for a bag of apples whether it's January or June, though the natural production of apples occurs in the fall. Grizzly bears have no way of storing or preserving food from season to season except as fat reserves. Thus, grizzly bears must eat what's available and in season.

When bears emerge from hibernation in the springtime, the annual foliage cycle is just beginning. Plants are starting to green up. The greening begins at lower elevations where the snow retreats more quickly, then moves upward to higher elevations as the season progresses. In spring and early summer, grizzly bears are usually found at the lower elevations within their range. They graze heavily upon newly emerging grasses. In most places bears recently arisen from their dens also scavenge the carcasses of winter-killed mammals. This food source and the species it involves vary depending on the area. In Yellowstone and Grand Teton National Parks, bison and elk carcasses are the two major sources of winter-killed carrion, although dead antelope, moose, and mule deer may also be found by a wandering bruin. In Alaska and Canada moose and caribou become increasingly important sources of after-winter carrion for grizzly bears.

Winter-killed animals are an important food source for grizzlies in some locations in early spring. Here a trio of bears feeds upon a bison carcass.

From late May through June, grizzlies exploit another source of protein. This period represents the birthing season for ungulates such as elk, deer, caribou, and moose. Grizzly bears are often very adept at discovering and killing newborn ungulates. Elk calves are especially prone to predation by bears in some areas. Cow elk tend to birth their young in the same places year after year in areas known as "calving grounds." Grizzly bears learn to frequent the calving grounds. Although elk calves are nearly scentless and well camouflaged, persistent grizzly bears consistently discover and dine upon the young in certain areas, especially in the northern Rocky Mountains, where elk are plentiful.

During the summer several seasonal trends affect the diet of grizzly bears. In the northern Rockies their access to meat declines as carrion is eaten and ungulate calves become too athletic to be easily captured. However, summer normally sprouts a robust and varied crop of plants. Grizzly bears typically ascend to alpine and subalpine meadows where they feed heavily upon plants and their roots. Bears inhabiting the coastal areas of British Columbia and Alaska descend to streams in midsummer where they dine enthusiastically upon spawning salmon. However, not all bears within traveling distance of spawning streams become fish-eaters. Some remain at high elevations, obtaining the highest percentage of their nutrition from alpine plants.

Locally, certain sources of what might best be described as "niche nutrition" become available to bears during the summer. In Yellowstone and Glacier National Parks, this includes the moths of the army cutworm. The moths show up during the summer among very high mountain slopes. Cutworm moths burrow into rockslides to avoid sunlight. Literally millions of moths may inhabit rockslides in the high country. Although they might not seem too appetizing to a human, moths pack a high punch of nutrition for bears, especially in the form of fat. Each moth contains around a half calorie of fat. It is estimated that an ambitious bear may consume in excess of 10,000 moths per day, with some estimates ranging as high as 40,000 moths per day. Thus, a moth-munching grizzly might easily consume 5,000 to 10,000 calories in a single day. Some biologists believe an enterprising grizzly that finds a bumper moth crop could account for nearly half of its yearly caloric requirements in a single month. However, the moth crop is highly variable. Some years they're abundant; at other times they're not.

In Yellowstone National Park spawning cutthroat trout were once an important summer protein source for several dozen grizzly bears in the Yellowstone Lake area. When the cutthroat trout moved upstream from Yellowstone Lake into spawning tributaries, they were preyed upon by bears that would stand in the small spawning streams. The bears usually caught the fish by squashing them against the stream bottom with their front paws. A researcher once observed a female grizzly catch and consume over one hundred cutthroat trout in a single day. Then in 1994 a fisherman caught a trout of a different species in Yellowstone Lake. Nonnative lake trout had evidently been illegally planted in the lake by humans. In a short period of time, the predatory lake trout decimated the cutthroat trout population in Yellowstone Lake. Currently, few cutthroats make the spawning run into Yellowstone Lake tributaries. This once-abundant source of early-summer protein for bears has all but vanished. Lake trout love deep water and do not require streams to spawn. Thus, the fish that now dominates Yellowstone Lake is inaccessible to grizzlies.

Late summer provides a caloric boost to foraging grizzly bears in many areas. At this time huckleberries, raspberries, chokecherries, rose hips, and other berries begin to ripen. Grizzly bears often descend to somewhat lower elevations at this time of year because berry bushes lower on the mountains produce their crop before those at higher altitudes.

Spawning cutthroat trout were once an important food source for grizzly bears in Yellowstone National Park, but have been displaced by nonnative lake trout.

Grizzly bears love to eat berries, such as chokecherries, huckleberries, and rose hips, in the late summer and early fall.

In the fall grizzly bears enter a period in their yearly life cycle known as "hyperphagia." Hyperphagia is a term used to describe overeating in humans. In relation to people chronic hyperphagia commonly leads to obesity and its related health problems. However, for grizzly bears hyperphagia isn't a dietary problem, it's a necessity. In late summer and autumn, bears enter a stage of hyperphagia where they eat ravenously. Weight gains by large bears during this feeding frenzy are impressive. A mature bear with access to abundant, high-calorie food sources can gain three to six pounds per day.

Grizzly bears commonly consume large quantities of fat- or sugar-laden foods during the fall, such as nuts and berries. The fall feeding strategy of a grizzly bear is very simple. Gorge on as much high-calorie food as possible to gain the fat reserves needed to maintain its body during several months of winter hibernation.

In years of plenty nature provides grizzly bears with all they need to satisfy their appetite during fall hyperphagia. However, in areas where berry crops are sparse or whitebark pines produce few nuts, autumn becomes a stressful time for bears seeking to accumulate the needed fat for winter. Hungry bears are more likely to raid camps and cabins seeking human food at this time. The potential for conflict with human hunters also increases. In many areas hunting seasons that allow people to kill moose, elk, deer, and other ungulates for their own consumption coincide with the hyperphagia stage of the grizzly's yearly feeding cycle. Grizzly bears may scavenge gut piles or carcasses from animals killed by human hunters, which sometimes results in deadly confrontations between these two-legged and four-legged predators. Bears with empty bellies are more likely to claim berry patches or frequent other food sources in areas of heavy human use during lean years, also increasing the odds of conflict with people. During this time bears living in areas that provide consistent sources of high-calorie foods buffered from high use by humans encounter the least amount of stress bulking up for hibernation.

CHAPTER 4 Abilities and Behavior

Physical Abilities

For many wildlife species their appearance gives some hint of their physical abilities. The lithe, streamlined form of the cheetah betrays its speed. The oversized hind legs of a jackrabbit suggest its ability to leap great distances. However, like some human athletes who don't quite look the part, grizzly bears are much faster and more agile than they appear. As noted earlier, grizzly bears can sprint as fast as the average horse and maintain a swift gait for several miles. Despite their lumbering appearance, should nature hold a North American track and field competition for

Grizzly bears are proficient swimmers and very comfortable in the water. Photo William Mullins

mammals, grizzlies could compete favorably as both sprinters and endurance runners. Grizzlies are also excellent swimmers and very comfortable in the water.

Along with their speed and swimming ability, grizzly bears are incredibly strong. I've watched foraging grizzly bears easily overturn rocks with a single jerk of a forepaw that I'm not sure I could so efficiently dislodge with the aid of a crowbar. Researchers in the mechanical engineering department at Montana State University once tested the strength of captive grizzly bears relative to humans. Grizzly bears commonly displayed strength equivalent to that of three to five humans under normal conditions. For example, the grizzly bears could easily roll over a 700-pound dumpster that it took two humans considerable effort just to tip over. The researchers also noted that if the grizzlies were enraged, their strength would be even more dramatic. Grizzly bears are reputed to have the ability to kill a moose or elk with a single blow of a forepaw. More readily observed is their dramatic strength in moving the carcasses of such animals. An adult grizzly bear can handily drag the carcass of an elk or caribou weighing 300 pounds or more should it decide it wants a change of scenery in its dining experience.

In addition to their bodily brawn, grizzly bears possess incredibly powerful jaws, estimated to have one of the highest crushing forces of any animal on the planet. A grizzly bear can break the large bones of its prey or carrion with its teeth to eat the nutritious marrow inside. An angry grizzly bear can sever the trunk of an evergreen tree several inches in diameter with a single bite. Researchers once found the skeletal remains of a large male black bear killed by a large male grizzly bear. The black bear's skull had been crushed by the jaws of the grizzly.

A certain amount of confusion surrounds the grizzly bear's ability to climb trees. Many people believe that black bears can climb trees but grizzly bears cannot. While it's true that black bears are much more efficient and agile tree-climbers than grizzlies, young grizzly bears can easily climb a tree. Adult grizzly bears seem much less inclined to climb, but most biologists believe they have the ability, especially in large trees with stout branches. Some literature erroneously claims that climbing a tree is a good way for humans to avoid a grizzly bear attack. However, grizzly bears have been known to climb trees in pursuit of humans. It's also important to remember that a standing adult grizzly bear can commonly reach 10 feet into a tree to grab an object with a front paw. In Denali National Park in Alaska, more than 10 percent of the documented bear-induced injuries to people have involved grizzlies pulling humans from trees.

Myths and misconceptions also pervade many people's understanding of grizzly bears' sensory abilities. The great brown bears are often described as creatures with a highly developed

Grizzly bears have a highly developed sense of smell. A grizzly bear's ability to detect odors probably rivals that of any animal in the world. Photo Kevin Rhoades

sense of smell, but possessed of poor eyesight and hearing. Only one aspect of this characterization is correct. Grizzly bears do have an incredibly developed sense of smell. The skull of a grizzly bear exhibits a notably large nasal cavity. Inside the cavity is a complex network of nasal mucus, roughly one hundred times larger than that of a human. In fact, smell is believed to be the grizzly bear's most highly developed sense. Estimates of ability vary, but many biologists feel a grizzly bear's sensitivity to odors is thousands of times more acute and sophisticated than that of a human.

Direct comparisons are difficult to establish, but a grizzly bear's sense of smell may be several times more acute than that of a bloodhound. Coastal grizzly bears in Alaska detect the presence of clams buried along the seashore by smelling them. Grizzly bears can smell carrion from several miles away. In addition to using their noses to find food, grizzly bears perceive much about one another based upon smell. By smelling urine or footprints, a male bear can learn much about another grizzly that's entered his home range, be it a female that he may court for mating or another male that might become a rival. Like some other animals, a grizzly bear has an additional scent-detecting organ on the roof of its mouth known as a Jacobson's organ. This organ detects scents borne by moisture and aids grizzly bears in communication with one another. Subordinate males can perceive the scent of a dominant bear and avoid it. Males use their olfactory senses to detect the presence of females and their readiness for breeding during the mating season.

Although a grizzly bear's sense of smell is assumed to be the most highly developed of its five senses, that doesn't mean its other perceptual abilities are stunted. Contrary to widespread belief, grizzly bears probably see just as well as humans. Grizzlies are often observed reacting to visual stimuli at considerable distances while hunting, just like a human might react to spotting a grizzly bear from a half mile away. Like other bears, grizzlies will often stand on their hind legs to make themselves taller. This behavior is not aggressive in nature. In most instances the bear is simply raising itself farther from the ground so that it can see better.

Grizzly bears are sometimes mistakenly characterized as having poor eyesight, but they see as well as humans. PHOTO WILLIAM MULLINS

A grizzly bear's night vision is superior to a person's. Bears have a reflective layer of tissue on the back of their eyeballs that bounces light back through the retina. This provides additional stimulation of the rods, the sensory portion of the eyeball responsible for night vision, increasing the bears' visual acuity in low light.

Little scientific information exists regarding the specific hearing abilities of grizzly bears or bears in general. It is believed by some biologists that bears have hearing abilities in the ultrasonic range, allowing them to detect sounds indiscernible to the human ear.

One research project involving polar bears demonstrated their ability and willingness to react to vocalizations of ringed seals, one of their primary prey. The ears of grizzly bears usually appear quite small in relation to their massive bodies, but this does not imply that their hearing ability is underdeveloped. Based upon numerous observations of grizzly bears, experts have concluded that their hearing is at least as acute as that of humans.

Tactile proficiency, or the sophisticated use of touch, might seem an ability far removed from the paws and jaws of a creature as big and brawny as a grizzly bear. However, grizzlies can adeptly work their claws into a crack between two rocks to gain leverage for unearthing a meal of grubs (or breaking into a garbage dumpster). "Bear-proof" food containers and garbage cans give ample evidence of grizzlies' dexterity with their paws. Such

Grizzly bears are very skillful in the use of their front paws and claws for grasping objects and digging. Photo William Mullins

containers must be carefully engineered so that an enterprising bear can't use its dexterous paws to access what's inside. Additional evidence of the grizzly bear's sophisticated sense of touch is found in their method for munching the nuts of whitebark pines. For decades biologists wondered how such large animals could effectively feed upon such small nuts. The riddle was answered when researchers gave captive bears some cones. The bears stomped and ripped the cones with their front paws to extract the nuts, then nimbly licked them up with their tongues!

Vocal and Visual Communication

Grizzly bears rely upon a wide variety of communication strategies. They "talk" to one another in sounds, although many of their vocalizations aren't easily heard from a distance. Females and cubs exchange vocal cues of their contentment and bond. Sows may grunt softly to their cubs. Cubs sometimes make a low noise indicating their security and contentment, similar to the purring sound of a cat. Young grizzlies still in the company of their mother may emit loud noises of distress that have the quality of bawling or screaming. Bears also blow air from their lungs as a means of vocalizing and make grunting sounds. Blowing and grunting can both be signs of apprehension or disturbance.

Loud, agitated huffing sounds are among those most strongly associated with aggression. Intense growling also communicates anger. Both of these sounds are highly significant to humans who accidentally encounter grizzly bears at close range. Huffing noises occurring just before a charge are reported by a high percentage of people who have been attacked by grizzly bears. Popping its jaws together is a similar means for a bear to communicate aggression.

Along with vocal indications, a bear's body language communicates its feelings. Grizzly bears standing on their hind legs are usually curious and merely attempting to get a better look at an object of attention. A bear that sits down is comfortable and at ease. When confronted by another bear, a human, or some other creature perceived as a threat, a grizzly bear may turn sideways or swing its head from side to side to indicate that it

Grizzly bears communicate with a variety of vocal and visual signals. Photo Lisa Densmore

feels threatened but is looking for a noncombative way out of the situation. Bears that stare another bear or animal directly in the eyes and lay back their ears feel threatened and may attack. This behavior can be accompanied by barks, moaning sounds, or woofing noises.

Grizzly bears also communicate in other ways. Bears use trees to communicate their presence to others of their kind. Grizzlies will rub their backs and shoulders on these "scratching posts," leaving behind a clear message in scent to other bears that wander into the area. They also mark the trees with their claws, often reaching high onto the trunk and scoring the bark deeply. These claw marks are thought to give other bears an indication of the health and strength of the individual marking the scratching post.

Hibernation

From late fall until spring, most grizzly bears retreat to dens below ground or dug into a snowbank to hibernate. On Alaska's Kodiak Island some males do not den at all. Elsewhere, denning behaviors generally follow predictable patterns. Females den before males in the fall and emerge later in the spring, making the total denning time for sows substantially longer than that of boars. Grizzly bears inhabiting northern climates have a longer denning period than those in the south. Thus, a male grizzly bear in Yellowstone National Park (latitude 44 degrees N) may spend around 130 days in its den, while a male in central Alaska (latitude 62 degrees N) may spend about 180 days in its winter dormancy.

Is "hibernation" the best descriptor of a bear's winter activity (or lack thereof)? In the past some biologists argued that bears are not true hibernators and their winter dormancy should be called "torpor" instead. However, most wildlife biologists now accept "hibernation" as the best description of this remarkable adaptation grizzly bears possess to avoid winter starvation. During hibernation bears do not eat, drink, or expel body waste. However, they do lose lots of weight. Remember all that fat bears try to gain during their fall feeding binges? A grizzly bear commonly drops 15 to 30 percent of its body mass during hibernation.

Hibernation in grizzly bears differs in some important ways from that experienced by other animals such as ground squirrels. These creatures, sometimes known as "deep hibernators," experience drastic decreases in body temperature. The body temperature of a deep hibernator may fall from over 100 degrees F to below 50 degrees F. Grizzly bears experience a much more modest reduction in body temperature of around 10 to 12 degrees F. A grizzly bear's metabolic rate drops to about one-half the rate of energy consumption when it is active at other times. A hibernating bear's heart rate may slow from forty-five beats per minute at rest during the summer to fifteen beats per minute during hibernation. Respirations can

GRIZZLY ISSUES

HIBERNATION AND HUMAN HEALTH

Two aspects of grizzly bear hibernation are of interest for human health researchers. First, although grizzly bears experience exceedingly high cholesterol levels during hibernation (twice as high as during the summer), they don't experience the arterial hardening that accompanies the same condition in humans. Hibernating bears also don't experience a reduction in bone mass. Other mammals that undergo long periods where they aren't bearing weight suffer from osteoporosis or a weakening of the bones. If researchers can pinpoint how bears avoid the negative effects of high cholesterol and maintain their bone density during hibernation, it might lead to improvements in health care for humans facing these conditions.

drop from seven breaths per minute to one breath every 45 seconds. Unlike deep hibernators that cannot be easily awakened or react in a coordinated manner to danger, hibernating grizzly bears can awaken quite quickly and are able to react efficiently when they do.

In most places grizzly bears dig their own dens. Some bears will use excavated dens for more than 1 year. Others utilize natural cavities such as caves for dens. In the far north bears sometimes dig dens into snowbanks. Location of denning sites varies with geographical region. However, some general trends exist. Dens are most often found on slopes that are steeper than others in an area. Grizzly bears prefer remote, undisturbed locations for their dens and are particularly vulnerable to disturbance at denning time. A grizzly bear surprised at its den may abandon the site.

Excavation of a den may involve a grizzly moving more than a ton of earth to create a winter home. It takes a grizzly about

3 to 7 days to dig a den. In terms of winter preparation, bears are just like people. Some folks put on their storm windows in advance; others wait until the last minute. Researchers have observed a similar pattern with grizzly bears. Some dig a den well in advance, while others don't do their excavating until shortly before retreating below ground for the winter.

In the yearly life cycle of the grizzly bear, another miraculous milestone occurs during hibernation. This is the time that sows give birth to their tiny, helpless cubs. But that's a story we'll save for the next chapter!

CHAPTER 5 Reproduction and Young

The Mating Season

Grizzly bear cubs are born to hibernating females in the dead of winter. But their life story actually begins the previous summer during the mating season. In late spring or early summer, male bears that are solitary during the rest of the year begin to seek and keep company with females. How do two grizzly bears, both of which might have a home range of several hundred square miles, find each other for mating? Scientists believe females of sufficient age and fitness for breeding leave scent trails in late spring that are discovered and followed by male bears. Once a male and female meet, they get acquainted. The prospective pair may engage in a game of chase, or wrestle. During these courtship activities the female is assessing the male's health and strength. If she finds him acceptable, the two will become a pair. Evidence of a female's acceptance of her suitor may be displayed by both bears through nuzzling and licking. These pair bonds, however, are short-lived, usually lasting a few days or weeks.

The time of actual breeding varies considerably depending on the location, the age and physical state of the female, and the particular year. A research study conducted in Yellowstone National Park reported the earliest date of breeding on May 18 and the latest on July 11. In Katmai National Park in Alaska, mating occurs from late May to early July. No matter where they live, most grizzly bears probably breed during the month of June.

During this time male bears will try to hide a female away from other males, keeping her in an isolated area where she's less likely to be seen or smelled by a rival. Grizzly bears are not monogamous, which means that during any given year a female may mate with more than one male and a male may mate with more than one female. Thus, a male bear will expend

Grizzly sows may mate with more than one boar. "Twin" cubs might actually have different fathers. Photo William Mullins

considerable energy trying to keep a female away from other males. In Waterton Lakes and Banff National Parks in Canada, researchers have documented boars essentially herding sows to high mountaintops. There they forcibly repel the female's attempts to return to lower elevations until breeding is complete. Evidently, some instinctual drive prompts them to isolate females in these lofty areas where their scent is much less likely to be dispersed to rival males.

In cases where a female mates with more than one male, each of the boars may father offspring in the same litter. Female grizzlies may produce up to four cubs in a litter, although one to three is most typical. In a litter of three, each of the cubs may be sired by a different father if the female mated with several different males during the breeding season. After breeding, a male may stay with a female for a short period of time. But by early August the pairs have normally broken up and bears of both sexes have gone back to their solitary ways.

Pregnancy and Gestation

For most mammals, whether a female becomes pregnant as a result of breeding is determined quickly. If the female's egg (or eggs) doesn't become fertilized and attach to the uterine wall shortly after mating, she will not become pregnant. This process, however, is much more complex for grizzly bears. Grizzly bears are one of a number of species (including other bears and animals such as weasels, armadillos, and seals) that become pregnant through a process known as "delayed implantation." Delayed implantation is an obligatory biological process for some species (such as grizzly bears), meaning it occurs all the time. In other species delayed implantation is a facultative process, referring to the fact that it occurs in response to conditions in a female's body or the environment.

After mating, fertilized eggs (embryos) float in a grizzly bear's uterus for a period of time. They remain viable during this interval, but do not absorb the nutrients from the female's body necessary for growth because they have not yet attached to the wall of the uterus. Sometime in late fall or early winter, about the time the sow enters her den, the embryos she is carrying either attach to the uterine wall, creating a pregnancy, or are simply reabsorbed by her body.

What determines whether a female bear becomes pregnant following the process of delayed implantation? Remember all that food grizzly bears eat in late summer and fall to store fat for hibernation? For female bears that mated earlier in the summer, fat reserves also play a critical role in pregnancy. If her body senses she has sufficient reserves of fat and other nutrients

A grizzly bear female won't become pregnant unless she has enough physical reserves for both hibernation and gestation. Photo William Mullins

necessary to successfully birth and nurse young, a sow will become pregnant. If not, her embryos will be reabsorbed by her body, delaying pregnancy for at least another year. Although it is a seemingly odd process, evolutionary biologists believe delayed implantation performs a necessary and beneficial function in grizzly bears. Gestation (the process of nourishing an embryo from implantation to birth) and nursing are costly biological processes for grizzly bear sows. By discontinuing a pregnancy when the female has insufficient physical reserves to either gestate or nurse her young, delayed implantation gives a measure of insurance to the reproductive process. In years that a female is in less than optimal body condition, she won't bear offspring, insulating both herself and her offspring from the risk of malnutrition.

If a female grizzly's body gives her pregnancy the green light, so to speak, the embryos attach to the uterine wall and begin to develop. Although the time between a female's mating and the birth of her cubs commonly spans 6 months or more, the actual gestation period is much shorter. From the time the embryo attaches to birth is about 8 weeks.

Birth

Grizzly cubs are born in January or February. Ironically, this is typically the coldest season of winter. Newborn cubs are extremely small and helpless in relation to the size and strength of an adult bear. They weigh less than a pound and enter the world blind, hairless, and without teeth. While birthing her cubs, the mother bear becomes semiconscious but quickly falls back into a deep sleep. The tiny cubs can move well enough to nurse, but are otherwise quite helpless. Growth occurs rapidly, however, due in large measure to the rich milk of the mother bear, which is more than 20 percent fat. By the time the cubs emerge from the den with their mother, their eyes are open, they have become very mobile, and their bodies are covered with fur. Although still very small, they've grown considerably, now weighing some six to nine pounds.

Nurturing Cubs to Adulthood

In general, sows with cubs are the last grizzly bears to awaken from hibernation in the spring. While the mother bear is still lethargic from her long winter's sleep, the cubs are playful and energetic. Females with young often stay close to the den site for several weeks and may sometimes temporarily return to the den for shelter.

For the first several months of life, grizzly bear cubs are highly dependent on their mother's milk for nourishment. Like adult bears, grizzly cubs are very intelligent. From an early age they are constantly observing their mother's behavior and mimic it with actions of their own. This pattern enables them to master skills

Grizzly bear females with new cubs are the last to emerge from their dens and may temporarily return to their dens for shelter. Photo Kevin Rhoades

they'll need in adulthood, such as feeding strategies. Cubs eat the foods their mother provides for them and quickly learn to find and harvest them on their own. Grizzly cubs also prepare for adult life with their seemingly boundless enthusiasm for play. Siblings from the same litter spend many hours wrestling on the ground or grappling while they stand upright on their hind legs. They like to chase one another or play what appears to be a game of follow-the-leader that may find them climbing on logs or scrambling over boulders.

More elaborate amusements are sometimes observed among individual cubs. In Yellowstone National Park I once observed a sow and her two yearling cubs scavenging an old bison carcass.

The carcass had decomposed to just a skeleton, but the mother and one of the cubs seemed quite content to gnaw on the bones. The other cub had a different agenda. Grasping a sizeable bone in its forepaws, it rolled onto its back and proceeded to toss the bone in the air. Thinking it a random but fascinating act, I grinned with delight at having the opportunity to observe and photograph such a unique, playful behavior. My delight turned to astonishment when the cub spent the next couple minutes deliberately tossing the bone aloft with its front paws and attempting to catch it. Such activities probably develop dexterity among young bears and also enhance their problem-solving skills. What's next? I thought as the bears finally ambled away. Is this youngster going to figure out how to juggle with bison bones?

Grizzly sows often nurture their cubs for 2 years after birth. These yearlings are nursing.

Young grizzly bears typically stay with their mother until they are 2 years old. As they age, they become increasingly less dependent upon the sow for care, although 2-year-old offspring have been observed nursing. Separation of mothers and their young may be triggered by her readiness to mate and produce another litter. Adult male grizzly bears are a persistent threat to cubs. For their first year of life, a grizzly sow will attempt to protect her cubs from an aggressive male. Grizzly bears can efficiently climb trees in their first year of life, a strategy they may use to elude the jaws of a threatening male. Scientists believe male bears may kill cubs for a variety of reasons. In some cases the cubs are eaten. Removing cubs from a female bear may also make her

Grizzly bears have one of the lowest reproductive rates of any North American mammal.
Photo William Mullins

Although she may only birth cubs every 3 years or more, a grizzly sow like this one in Yellowstone National Park can successfully raise cubs to age 20.

more apt to breed. It has also been theorized that boars kill cubs that have been sired by other males, increasing the likelihood that young in a particular area are the offspring of the dominant male. Whatever the motivation, adult males of their own kind are one of the hazards cubs must avoid in order to reach adulthood.

The fact that grizzly sows normally invest what amounts to 3 years from the time they breed until their cubs depart and they breed again is one of the reasons grizzlies have one of the lowest reproductive rates of any North American mammal. Another factor involves their slow pace toward sexual maturity. Grizzly bear females normally become capable of reproduction at between 4 and 7 years of age. Males usually reach sexual maturity at 4 to 6 years of age.

The age at which a female births her first litter and becomes part of the reproducing population of grizzly bears varies substantially by region. Nutrition plays a big factor in when a grizzly sow is able to produce her first litter. Bears on the Alaskan Peninsula, where food is abundant, often birth their first litter at 4 or 5 years of age. In Yellowstone National Park the average age of first reproduction for females averages around 6 years of age. Areas that offer bears poorer access to nutritious forage may see few females reproducing until they are 7 or 8 years old. Once they reach breeding age, sow grizzlies may produce young until they are 20 years old or more. Given the grizzly bear's slow rate of sexual maturity and reproduction, the loss of even a few breeding-age females in a small population may greatly reduce its viability.

CHAPTER 6 Grizzly Bears and Other Animals

Grizzlies and Other Predators

Grizzly bears are often referred to as "top-of-the-food-chain predators." Such a characterization is correct. I've found Internet chats debating the outcome of a fight between a grizzly bear and a lion or male gorilla. But under wild, natural conditions, precious few rival predators will challenge the supremacy of a grizzly bear. In eastern Russia, Siberian tigers are known to kill members of the *Ursus arctos* species (and vice versa). Conflicts between grizzly bears and polar bears may find the great white hunters of the north gaining the upper hand. Wolverines are believed capable of usurping or defending a carcass from a grizzly bear, primarily through a frightful display of snarling and intimidation. But with very rare exceptions, no single wild animal that shares its habitat deliberately challenges an adult grizzly bear.

Nonetheless, grizzly bears in many habitats maintain complex and important relationships with other predators. The relationship between wolves and grizzly bears is particularly intriguing. In Alaska and Canada interactions between grizzly bears and wolves have continued their natural course for centuries. In the lower forty-eight states, however, wolves were exterminated a century ago. The reintroduction of wolves to Yellowstone National Park and the natural colonization of wolves in Glacier National Park and other portions of the northern Rocky Mountains in the contiguous United States have necessitated that indigenous grizzly bear populations once again accommodate wolves in their world.

In Yellowstone researchers have had ample opportunity to observe interactions between grizzly bears and the recently returned wolves. From the standpoint of grizzlies, wolves

Undisputed rulers of their world, grizzly bears are only in rare instances deliberately challenged by other predators. Photo William Mullins

represent both opportunity and opposition. Prior to wolf reintroduction management biologists theorized that winter wolf predation would leave fewer carcasses of winter-killed ungulates (primarily elk and bison) available for scavenging by grizzly bears in the early spring. However, they also postulated that this diminished presence of a potentially important food source might be offset by grizzly bears taking over carcasses of animals killed by wolves. Some concern was expressed regarding the possibility of wolf packs killing young grizzly bear cubs.

In general, biologists' predictions regarding wolf and grizzly bear interactions in Yellowstone were accurate and reflect the

In many places such as Yellowstone National Park, wolves and grizzly bears share a complex relationship that may ultimately be very beneficial to bears. Photo Kevin Rhoades

relationship between the two species in Alaska, Canada, and other places where wolves and grizzlies share the same range. Adult grizzly bears in Yellowstone are usually successful in usurping carcasses from wolves, but not always. Female bears with cubs are frequently repelled by wolves, possibly for the cubs' protection. Wolves and grizzly bears have also been observed peaceably feeding on the same carcass.

Do the two species kill one another? The short answer is yes. In 2001, 6 years after wolves were reintroduced to Yellowstone, researchers discovered the carcasses of two grizzly bear cubs in separate locations. Both were killed near animal carcasses (one an elk, the other a bison) that had been fed upon by both grizzly bears and wolves. Laboratory analysis of the dead cubs indicated both had been killed by wolves.

The status of interactions between wolves and grizzly bears in Yellowstone is essentially similar to those observed elsewhere. Grizzly cubs are in the greatest danger from wolves. Wolves take their greatest risk when attempting to defend a carcass from an adult grizzly bear. Den sites of wolves are vigorously protected by the pack. Wolf packs are highly successful repelling grizzlies from their denning areas. However, black bears are known to have killed single female wolves defending a den, so a similar outcome from an aggressive grizzly bear is also possible. Biologists seem to agree that where prey animals are abundant, competition between wolves and grizzly bears is negligible. Where prey is less plentiful, the presence of the two species may exert some influence on the populations of each other, but such a relationship is difficult to establish. For wildlife watchers the rare opportunity to view wolves and grizzly bears in the same setting or observe their infrequent interactions with each other is a thrill not soon to be forgotten.

Interactions between wolves and grizzly bears are not commonplace. But due to the fact that both of these predators frequent open country, these interactions are more easily observed by humans than interactions between grizzlies and more seldom seen predators, such as mountain lions (cougars).

Black bears generally give grizzlies a wide berth and may climb a tree for protection, as grizzlies will seldom expend the effort to follow them into a tree.

Mountain lions are rarely viewed by humans in the wild. As they prefer habitats with timber or shrub cover and are highly nocturnal creatures with incredible eyesight, the odds of a person sighting a mountain lion in uncontrolled outdoor settings is very low. Thus, directly observing behavioral exchanges between grizzly bears and mountain lions is like uncovering a needle in the proverbial haystack.

Nonetheless, researchers have discovered a potentially very important relationship between mountain lions and grizzly bears. Researchers in the northern Rocky Mountains of the United States have documented grizzly bears displacing cougars from their kills with a surprising frequency. In one study researchers found that of fifteen cougar-killed elk in the Kintla Lake region of Glacier National Park, grizzly bears visited 33 percent, or five of the kills. Mountain lions in several study areas routinely lost carcasses to grizzly bears. Grizzlies usurping cougar kills happens most frequently in the fall and early spring, when the two animals both tend to live in proximity to elk and deer, two of the most common prey species of mountain lions.

At least in some locations, it appears that stealing carcasses from cougars may be a significant way for grizzlies to access high-protein, nutritious forage at times when they most need it. Prior to denning and just after emergence are two times of the year when discovering abundant food sources is very beneficial to bears, and these are the times when they're most likely to obtain carcasses from mountain lions. However, the situation isn't so advantageous for the cats. When a grizzly bear moves in on a mountain lion's kill, the cat is forced to attempt a defense of its prey or make another kill. Predation is a high-risk endeavor for cougars. A study in Alberta, Canada, indicated that almost 30 percent of the natural deaths to cougars were a result of wounds sustained while attempting to kill prey. Researchers once observed an exceptionally skilled team of mountain lion hunters consisting of a female and her two large cubs. In 23 days this hunting team killed four elk, two cows, and two large calves. Grizzly bears displaced the cougars from one of the kills and fed on two others. Biologists estimated that the bears gleaned nearly 350 pounds of food from these carcasses. Where grizzly bears and cougars share the same range, the bears may receive substantial benefit from the mountain lions. The cougars, by contrast, may experience more risk and adversity from the bears.

Grizzlies also share their world with other bears, polar and black. Interactions between grizzly and polar bears were discussed in Chapter 1, but what about black bears? In general, black bears give grizzly bears a wide berth. Large male black bears may effectively compete with subadult grizzly bears, but otherwise the dominance of grizzlies over their smaller, black cousins is obvious and rarely challenged. Grizzly bears may attempt to kill black bears, but in these infrequent instances the black bears' climbing ability gives them an advantage. An adult grizzly bear is unlikely to expend the effort to try to dislodge a black bear from a tree it has climbed for protection. However, researchers have documented black bear deaths at the jaws of grizzlies.

Parasites and Diseases

Grizzly bears, like other free-roaming mammals, commonly encounter a range of parasites. These include external parasites (such as ticks and fleas) and internal parasites (such as tapeworms and roundworms). The role of parasites in relation to grizzly bears' health and reproductive efficiency is not clearly understood. But researchers believe that the nutritional stress caused by parasites that has been well documented with other species also affects grizzly bears. Various habitats and locations determine the extent to which grizzly bears might be exposed to parasites. Some parasites are common in certain portions of grizzly bear range but absent in others.

A survey of grizzly bears in western Montana and Yellowstone National Park discovered nine various parasites afflicting grizzlies, from wood ticks to hookworms. It is assumed that grizzlies inhabiting similar habitats in Idaho, Washington, and the Canadian Rockies would be exposed to similar parasites. Roundworms were the mostly commonly occurring parasite, followed by trichina worms, tapeworms, and hookworms. Most of these are intestinal parasites, except for the trichina worm, which invades its host's tissue. Forty percent of the cubs surveyed were host to parasites, a figure that climbed to over 90 percent in 6- to 9-year-old bears. Grizzly bears surveyed in the Northwest Territories of Canada were also commonly afflicted with intestinal parasites, especially roundworms and tapeworms.

Healthy, adult grizzly bears probably don't experience severely negative effects from internal parasites in low concentrations. However, in high concentrations intestinal parasites may rob significant levels of nutrition from grizzly bears. Some species of tapeworms absorb high quantities of vitamin B12 from humans, resulting in anemia, but the extent to which this occurs in bears is unknown. Large numbers of intestinal parasites rob nutrition from their host, an occurrence that may influence the health of infected grizzly bears. In 2010 a female grizzly bear killed one camper and injured two others at a campground near Cooke City, Montana. She fed upon the individual she killed. The attack was most probably motivated by hunger. The sow was accompanied by three cubs and in very poor physical condition, her small intestine loaded with parasites. It is impossible to explain the exact reason for such a deadly attack, but experts believe her severe malnutrition, exacerbated by parasites, probably prompted the attacks.

Predation

Grizzly bears consume a mostly vegetarian diet in most places, yet their ability as predators is considerable. In certain areas of Yellowstone National Park, grizzly bears prey upon a higher percentage of elk calves than any other predator, including wolves. In a 2003 to 2005 study in Yellowstone, bears (black and grizzly) accounted for around 55 to 60 percent of the entire mortality of tagged calves in the study. The keen noses of grizzly bears and their intelligence and stamina make them very effective predators of elk calves. Elk birth their young in the same areas year after year. Grizzlies remember these places and use their hunting skills

Grizzly bears are capable predators, commonly targeting the young of species such as elk, deer, moose, and caribou, but are also capable of killing adult animals.

in several strategies to kill young elk. When elk calves are very young, grizzlies will cover a known calving area in a zigzagging pattern. They use their keen sense of smell to locate the nearly scentless calves, but also periodically rear on their hind legs to visually search for calves. Grizzlies also ambush bands of elk cows and calves in open areas, seeking to confuse and separate young calves from the herd. The young elk are often caught by a bear that cuts them off when they attempt to rejoin the herd. Ambush tactics are also used by grizzly bears that stalk within close range of elk calves using timber or other cover, then rush quickly to make their kill. Finally, grizzlies will occasionally use their speed and stamina to capture young elk. Researchers once observed a grizzly bear chasing a herd of elk for over 30 minutes in a chase that covered almost 2 miles, killing three elk calves in the process. Newborn caribou, moose, and deer are likewise primary prey animals for grizzlies in areas where they exist.

Young ungulates aren't the only ones killed by grizzlies. Under the right circumstances grizzly bears can and do prey upon adult animals. Grizzly predation on mature ungulates usually occurs in the spring, when bears are able to target animals weakened by the winter. They also opportunistically hunt hoofed animals that have been injured or are otherwise vulnerable. In rare instances

The predatory efforts of grizzlies aren't always focused on large animals; although seldom successful, they may even chase birds such as ducks and geese. Photo William Mullins

grizzly bears successfully hunt and kill healthy adult ungulates, even bison, the largest hoofed animal in North America. In the fall of 2000, a researcher observed a sow grizzly bear successfully bring to earth a 3-year-old bull bison.

The predation efforts of grizzly bears aren't always targeted on large animals. They routinely dig small, burrowing animals such as pocket gophers from the earth. Grizzlies have been observed chasing ducks, geese, and sandhill cranes. To my knowledge, no one has seen a grizzly bear actually catching a bird, but such an outcome isn't outside the realm of possibility, given the remarkable physical abilities of these great, athletic predators.

CHAPTER 7 Grizzly Bears and Humans

Grizzly Bears in History

The awe, fear, and fascination that modern people find in the grizzly bear were shared by many ancient peoples. Evidence of the dominant place the grizzly bear held in the lore and legends of our historical predecessors is amply illustrated in stories concerning stars. The name of the constellation Ursa Major means "great bear." Ancient Greeks identified the stars of this constellation forming the shape of a bear. A legend concerning Zeus, the ruler of the gods, accompanied it. Zeus fell in love with a nymph, Callisto, who bore him a child. Zeus's wife, Hera, was jealous and transformed Callisto into a bear. Later Callisto's child, who had become a hunter, was about to inadvertently kill his mother. Zeus intervened, tossing both the bear-mother and her son into the sky, where they became the constellations Ursa Major and Ursa Minor. In the two constellations the "bears" have very long tails, unlike flesh-and-blood grizzly bears on earth. Evidently, Zeus used the long tails as handles for casting the bears into the sky.

Independently of the Greeks, American Indian peoples generated their own legends of a great bear in the sky. While the Greeks identified the bear with the entire constellation of Ursa Major, American Indians saw the bear in the stars of the Big Dipper. Technically speaking, the Big Dipper is not a constellation, but an obvious grouping of stars, known in the astronomical world as an "asterism." An asterism is a smaller, more easily recognized portion of a constellation. Various American Indian tribes viewed the Big Dipper as a great bear (most likely a grizzly) being pursued by three hunters. The four stars composing the "cup" portion of the Big Dipper are the bear; the three stars composing the "handle" part of the asterism are the hunters. Throughout the seasons the movements of the Big Dipper across the northern sky recount a story of the interactions between the hunters and the hunted. The hunters discover the bear in the spring. All summer they pursue the

Various American Indian legends equate the Big Dipper with a grizzly bear. PHOTO SHUTTERSTOCK

bear across the night sky. In the fall they catch up to it and pierce it with their arrows. The bear rises on its hind feet, staining the earth with its blood, which corresponds to the red coloration in autumn foliage. All winter it is laid low in death, but as hibernating bears of the earth disappear below ground in late fall only to reappear in the spring, the great bear in the sky is also reborn. The story of the hunt is replayed every year in the movements of the Big Dipper across the night sky. Various tribes told differing versions of the story. Some replaced humans hunting the great bear with birds. Of the birds pursuing the grizzly bear, it was the robin that killed it, forever staining the feathers on its breast with the blood of the bear. This is why robins have a red breast.

In addition to the dramatic story staged in the heavens, American Indian tribes recounted numerous other legends regarding the grizzly bear, stories that involved the grizzly bear in relation to other animals as well as humans. Throughout the legends one dominant theme persists. The grizzly bear is the mightiest of the animals and very intelligent as well. Both humans and other animals are wise to remember this and give the bear its due respect.

The American Indians' reverence toward the grizzly bear showed in activities other than their legends. Plains Indians felt that the powers of the grizzly bear, if appropriated by people, could guard warriors in battle and cure or insulate individuals from illness. Native peoples of the Pacific Northwest commonly adorned totem poles, dishes, and other items with images of bears. Hunters from some tribes pursued and killed grizzly bears as a sign of a warrior's exceptional courage and skill. Grizzly bear claws and hides decorated the clothing of some tribes, and the meat of a grizzly bear would be consumed as well. Other groups left bears alone, prohibiting the eating of bear meat.

Grizzly Bears in Modern Times

As described in Chapter 2, the arrival of European immigrants to North American and their settling of the West dramatically reduced the range of grizzly bears. A few bears persisted in places as far south as California in the 1920s, but bears were eliminated from all but a few areas shortly thereafter. One of the strongholds of the grizzly bear was Yellowstone National Park, a place whose history with bears suggestively illustrates changing attitudes of Americans toward grizzly bears and the natural world over time. When Yellowstone was created in 1872 through an act of Congress, it preserved a large region of habitat from logging, agriculture, settlement, and other human activities that brought people in conflict with grizzlies. However, human interactions with grizzlies in the early decades of Yellowstone weren't always in the bears' best interest. By the early 1890s grizzly bears had joined black bears in scavenging garbage from open-pit dumps adjacent to lodging facilities and campgrounds, developing an association with humans and food. In 1916 the first documented human fatality occurred in the park. A grizzly bear killed a wagon driver and raided his load of oats and hay. In response, associates of the teamster baited a barrel filled with dynamite. When the bear came to the trap, the charge was detonated, blowing up the bear.

People viewing captive grizzly bears can falsely conclude that they're oversized pets. This grizzly was photographed as part of a streetside animal act in Moscow, Russia, in 2000. Such portrayals have become less common in the United States in the past several decades and are highly discouraged by grizzly bear experts.

By the 1950s bears begging along the park's roadsides, both grizzly bears and black bears, were a major tourist attraction in Yellowstone. Visitors hand-fed bears from their vehicles, sometimes getting clawed in the process. Bears damaged automobiles and camps. While most visitors viewed Yellowstone's food-scavenging bears as a novelty, others saw them as a nuisance. Cartoon portrayals, circus acts, and other uses of bears for entertainment purposes during this time (and sometimes persisting into the present) often portrayed bears more along the lines of overgrown pets or cuddly characters than wild and potentially dangerous animals that are never truly tamed.

A grizzly bear researcher snapped this photo of a sow grizzly and three cubs raiding a dumpster at night. Such instances led to the development of bear-proof storage for garbage and food in national parks and other areas. Photo Kevin Rhoades

Recognizing the need for greater self-sufficiency in the grizzly bear population and charting a new management course to return bears to their natural mode of living, Yellowstone National Park enacted a series of management plans from the 1960s to the mid-1980s that closed dumps, vigorously enforced prohibitions on bear feeding, and created food storage regulations for campers. At first grizzly bears had a difficult time readjusting. However, conflicts and necessary removal of "problem bears" began to diminish as new generations of grizzlies, no longer dependent upon human food sources, were born. Although the specifics varied in different locations, a similar evolution of bear management and conservation also occurred in such locations as Glacier National Park, Canadian parks, and popular bear-viewing areas in Alaska.

In 1975 grizzly bears in the contiguous United States were designated a threatened species under the provisions of the Endangered Species Act. As such, grizzly bears are protected from hunting in the lower forty-eight states. Land-use practices in grizzly bear habitat must also conform to certain measures of conservation for bears.

In Alaska and Canada grizzly bears are protected in some areas, but can be hunted by humans in others. Grizzly bear hunting is closely regulated and monitored, with quotas intended to protect populations from decline due to overhunting. Although some advocacy groups believe grizzly bears should never be hunted, wildlife managers in Alaska and Canada believe that regulated hunting does not represent a significant risk to grizzly bear numbers.

Humans and Bears: Current Interactions and Precautions

The thought of being attacked by a grizzly bear is enough to keep some people from recreating in bear habitat or may leave them shivering in their sleeping bag or constantly looking over their shoulders for a ghost bear when hiking. However, statistics reveal that this fear, while potentially a strong motivator for taking precautions that protect both bears and people, is unfounded.

As many outdoor folks are fond of quipping, you're probably at greater danger from dying in an automobile accident on the way to the trailhead than encountering the jaws of an enraged grizzly while on the trail. Dogs and lightning strikes both kill more people per year, on average, than grizzly bears. Nonetheless, grizzly bears do occasionally attack and kill people. In some years several deaths have occurred in the contiguous United States in a single season of grizzly activity, from the time of their emergence from their dens in the spring until they hibernate in the winter.

Certain scenarios greatly increase the odds of a grizzly attacking a human. Hunters are often at much higher risk than hikers or other backcountry users. The tactics used by human hunters to control their scent, walk quietly to avoid detection

Hunters surprising grizzly bears in cover at close range is a common cause of grizzly attacks on humans.

Grizzly bears may attack humans when defending a carcass. If you see or smell carrion in grizzly country, exit the area immediately. Photo William Mullins

by their quarry, and hide from sight up the odds of surprising a grizzly bear at close range. In some areas grizzly bears seem to have associated rifle shots and human activity in the fall with food in the form of discarded entrails and carcasses. A hunter returning to a kill site to retrieve meat from an animal may come upon a grizzly bear that has claimed the carcass and aggressively defends it. While human hunters encounter risk from inadvertently provoking a grizzly bear, bears are also at risk from hunters. In many places legal black bear hunting takes place in grizzly habitat. Grizzly bears being misidentified and downed by black bear hunters is a common occurrence.

The same behavior (defending a carcass) that may provoke conflict between hunters and grizzly bears also puts other recreationists at risk. Hikers or backcountry anglers may accidentally stray close to a carcass being eaten by a grizzly bear, triggering an aggressive response. When in grizzly bear habitat, if you see or smell carrion, it's wise to back out of the area the way you came and either give the location a wide berth or take your recreation elsewhere.

Females with cubs are considered the grizzly bears most likely to attack people, and such defensive measures by sows account for a high percentage of injurious or fatal conflicts. The typical scenario involves a person (or persons) who unexpectedly

Grizzly sows with cubs are considered the most dangerous of all bears to humans. When recreating in bear country, make lots of noise to avoid surprising bears and be especially vigilant in areas with limited sight range.

encounters a sow with cubs at close range or comes between a sow and her cubs. Making noise while hiking or recreating in grizzly habitat, avoiding heavy cover, and being especially vigilant while entering areas (such as ridgetops) where you might have trouble sensing bears and vice versa will greatly reduce the possibility of encountering this potentially deadly scenario.

Despite people's best attempts to avoid a confrontation with a grizzly bear, attacks may still occur. Experts offer several suggestions for surviving a grizzly attack. Bear-pepper spray, a substance derived from the stinging oil of hot pepper, has a proven record as a bear repellent. The spray is contained in pressurized canisters. During an attack the user sprays the contents of the canister in the bear's face at close range. The spray causes a burning sensation to the membranes of the bear's face and nasal passages, similar to the effects in a human struck with tear gas (or pepper spray).

In the absence of bear-pepper spray or if it fails to repel a charging bear, experts advise individuals to "play dead." This involves lying facedown on the ground, using your arms and hands to shield your head and neck. If wearing a pack, leave it on. The pack helps protect your back from bites or clawing. In most cases an aggressive grizzly is simply attempting to show a human who is boss or eliminate a perceived threat from its environment. Many biologists feel that even in fatal attacks, the grizzly's actions aren't specifically designed to kill a person, just to rough it up a bit to send a message. However, even a "disciplinary" swat or bite from an animal that can kill a large ungulate with a single snap of its jaws or blow from its paws can be fatal to a human. By playing dead you're communicating to the bear that you aren't a threat. After the bear leaves remain on the ground as long as you can. If you move too soon, the bear might renew the attack if it hasn't left the area.

While the prospect of being mauled by a grizzly is terrifying, bear experts believe the vast majority of attacks can be avoided. In addition to the precautions noted above, individuals should take extreme care to store food and other items that might draw grizzly bears when camping in bear country. Most developed

Grizzly bears need personal space and habitat protection to thrive in the world they share with humans. Photo William Mullins

or backcountry campsites in national parks offer bear-proof containers for storing food or elevated poles that allow food to be hung out of reach of bears. No matter where you camp in grizzly country, food and other items potentially attractive to bears should never be kept in a tent and should be stored well away from your campsite. These items include toothpaste, skin creams, some soaps, and other items not normally perceived as food.

Magnificent icons of wilderness, grizzly bears afforded their proper respect are far less likely to claim the life of a human than many other creatures and occurrences that we don't normally regard as dangerous. Grizzly bears need both personal space and large expanses of untrammeled habitat to healthily coexist with humans. In offering it to them, it seems we improve our own world as well.

AUTHOR'S NOTE: The above suggestions about how to avoid and survive a grizzly bear attack are provided only as very general guidelines. For more specific details please refer to information provided by the national parks or other government agencies. Or pick up a copy of the FalconGuides *Bear Aware* by Bill Schneider, an excellent book with comprehensive information for individuals in grizzly and black bear country.

Index

About the Author

A writer, photographer, and naturalist, Jack Ballard is a frequent contributor to numerous regional and national publications. He covers a variety of outdoor, conservation, and wildlife topics. He has written hundreds of articles on wildlife and wildlife-related topics (including grizzly bears) that have appeared in such magazines as *Colorado Outdoors, Camping Life, Wyoming Wildlife,* and many others. Jack also blogs on wildlife topics for Audubon Guides.

His photos have been published in numerous books (Smithsonian Press and Heinemann Library, for example), calendars, and magazines. Jack has received multiple awards for his writing and photography from the Outdoor Writers Association of America and other professional organizations. He holds two master's degrees and is an accomplished public speaker, entertaining students, conference attendees, and recreation/conservation groups with his compelling narratives. When not wandering the backcountry, he hangs his hat in Red Lodge, Montana. See more of his work at www.jackballard.com.